The DEFINITIVE guide to Democratic Party accomplishments in the Trump era

2020 Election Special Edition

By Kamala Warren

Copyright 2019 Kamala Warren. All rights reserved

ISBN 978-1-7334381-0-0

Cover illustration by Marietjie Opperman on Dreamstime.com

Disclaimer: After carrying out untold hours of exhaustive investigation with the intent of providing a definitive guide on the subject, it is to the best of the author's knowledge that all of the information presented in this is book is both accurate and properly attributed – hence, all of the pages are blank.

Saint Grobian Press

Stalingrad – Toronto – Uruguay – Potomac – Inglewood - Detroit

Check out our other great products at:

www.UnionOfTruth.org

Other books by Kamala Warren:

1- The DEFINITIVE Guide to Facts and Logic that Justify Sanctuary Cities

2- The DEFINITIVE Guide to Fact-based Justification for Homosexual Indoctrination of Kindergarten Students

3- The DEFINITIVE Guide to Facts and Logic that Justify Government-Run Healthcare

4- The DEFINITIVE Guide to Facts and Logic that Justify Disarming Law-Abiding Citizens

5- The DEFINITIVE Guide to Facts and Logic that Justify Mandatory Usage of Preferred Pronouns

6- The DEFINITIVE Guide to Facts and Logic that Justify Universal Basic Income

7- The DEFINITIVE Guide to Trump's Hate-Filled, Racist Remarks

8- The DEFINITIVE Guide to Trump's Treasonous Collusion and Obstruction

9- The DEFINITIVE Guide to Fact-based Justification for Spying on Candidate Trump

10- The DEFINITIVE Guide to Fact-based Justification for Trump's Impeachment

11- The DEFINITIVE Guide to Cogent Liberal Talking Points

The DEFINITIVE guide to Democratic Party
accomplishments in the Trump era

The DEFINITIVE guide to Democratic Party
accomplishments in the Trump era

The DEFINITIVE guide to Democratic Party
accomplishments in the Trump era

The DEFINITIVE guide to Democratic Party
accomplishments in the Trump era

The DEFINITIVE guide to Democratic Party
accomplishments in the Trump era

The DEFINITIVE guide to Democratic Party
accomplishments in the Trump era

The DEFINITIVE guide to Democratic Party
accomplishments in the Trump era

The DEFINITIVE guide to Democratic Party
accomplishments in the Trump era

The DEFINITIVE guide to Democratic Party
accomplishments in the Trump era

The DEFINITIVE guide to Democratic Party
accomplishments in the Trump era

The DEFINITIVE guide to Democratic Party
accomplishments in the Trump era

The DEFINITIVE guide to Democratic Party
accomplishments in the Trump era

The DEFINITIVE guide to Democratic Party
accomplishments in the Trump era

The DEFINITIVE guide to Democratic Party
accomplishments in the Trump era

The DEFINITIVE guide to Democratic Party
accomplishments in the Trump era

The DEFINITIVE guide to Democratic Party
accomplishments in the Trump era

The DEFINITIVE guide to Democratic Party
accomplishments in the Trump era

The DEFINITIVE guide to Democratic Party
accomplishments in the Trump era

The DEFINITIVE guide to Democratic Party
accomplishments in the Trump era

The DEFINITIVE guide to Democratic Party
accomplishments in the Trump era

The DEFINITIVE guide to Democratic Party
accomplishments in the Trump era

The DEFINITIVE guide to Democratic Party
accomplishments in the Trump era

The DEFINITIVE guide to Democratic Party
accomplishments in the Trump era

The DEFINITIVE guide to Democratic Party
accomplishments in the Trump era

The DEFINITIVE guide to Democratic Party
accomplishments in the Trump era

The DEFINITIVE guide to Democratic Party
accomplishments in the Trump era

The DEFINITIVE guide to Democratic Party
accomplishments in the Trump era

The DEFINITIVE guide to Democratic Party
accomplishments in the Trump era

The DEFINITIVE guide to Democratic Party
accomplishments in the Trump era

The DEFINITIVE guide to Democratic Party
accomplishments in the Trump era

The DEFINITIVE guide to Democratic Party
accomplishments in the Trump era

The DEFINITIVE guide to Democratic Party
accomplishments in the Trump era

The DEFINITIVE guide to Democratic Party
accomplishments in the Trump era

The DEFINITIVE guide to Democratic Party
accomplishments in the Trump era

The DEFINITIVE guide to Democratic Party
accomplishments in the Trump era

The DEFINITIVE guide to Democratic Party
accomplishments in the Trump era

The DEFINITIVE guide to Democratic Party
accomplishments in the Trump era

The DEFINITIVE guide to Democratic Party
accomplishments in the Trump era

The DEFINITIVE guide to Democratic Party
accomplishments in the Trump era

The DEFINITIVE guide to Democratic Party
accomplishments in the Trump era

The DEFINITIVE guide to Democratic Party
accomplishments in the Trump era

The DEFINITIVE guide to Democratic Party
accomplishments in the Trump era

The DEFINITIVE guide to Democratic Party
accomplishments in the Trump era

The DEFINITIVE guide to Democratic Party
accomplishments in the Trump era

The DEFINITIVE guide to Democratic Party
accomplishments in the Trump era

The DEFINITIVE guide to Democratic Party
accomplishments in the Trump era

The DEFINITIVE guide to Democratic Party
accomplishments in the Trump era

The DEFINITIVE guide to Democratic Party
accomplishments in the Trump era

The DEFINITIVE guide to Democratic Party
accomplishments in the Trump era

The DEFINITIVE guide to Democratic Party
accomplishments in the Trump era

The DEFINITIVE guide to Democratic Party
accomplishments in the Trump era

The DEFINITIVE guide to Democratic Party
accomplishments in the Trump era

The DEFINITIVE guide to Democratic Party
accomplishments in the Trump era

The DEFINITIVE guide to Democratic Party
accomplishments in the Trump era

The DEFINITIVE guide to Democratic Party
accomplishments in the Trump era

The DEFINITIVE guide to Democratic Party
accomplishments in the Trump era

The DEFINITIVE guide to Democratic Party
accomplishments in the Trump era

The DEFINITIVE guide to Democratic Party
accomplishments in the Trump era

The DEFINITIVE guide to Democratic Party
accomplishments in the Trump era

The DEFINITIVE guide to Democratic Party
accomplishments in the Trump era

The DEFINITIVE guide to Democratic Party
accomplishments in the Trump era

The DEFINITIVE guide to Democratic Party
accomplishments in the Trump era

The DEFINITIVE guide to Democratic Party
accomplishments in the Trump era

The DEFINITIVE guide to Democratic Party
accomplishments in the Trump era

The DEFINITIVE guide to Democratic Party
accomplishments in the Trump era

The DEFINITIVE guide to Democratic Party
accomplishments in the Trump era

The DEFINITIVE guide to Democratic Party
accomplishments in the Trump era

The DEFINITIVE guide to Democratic Party
accomplishments in the Trump era

The DEFINITIVE guide to Democratic Party
accomplishments in the Trump era

The DEFINITIVE guide to Democratic Party
accomplishments in the Trump era

The DEFINITIVE guide to Democratic Party
accomplishments in the Trump era

The DEFINITIVE guide to Democratic Party
accomplishments in the Trump era

The DEFINITIVE guide to Democratic Party
accomplishments in the Trump era

The DEFINITIVE guide to Democratic Party
accomplishments in the Trump era

The DEFINITIVE guide to Democratic Party
accomplishments in the Trump era

The DEFINITIVE guide to Democratic Party
accomplishments in the Trump era

The DEFINITIVE guide to Democratic Party
accomplishments in the Trump era

The DEFINITIVE guide to Democratic Party
accomplishments in the Trump era

The DEFINITIVE guide to Democratic Party
accomplishments in the Trump era

The DEFINITIVE guide to Democratic Party
accomplishments in the Trump era

The DEFINITIVE guide to Democratic Party
accomplishments in the Trump era

The DEFINITIVE guide to Democratic Party
accomplishments in the Trump era

The DEFINITIVE guide to Democratic Party
accomplishments in the Trump era

The DEFINITIVE guide to Democratic Party
accomplishments in the Trump era

The DEFINITIVE guide to Democratic Party
accomplishments in the Trump era

The DEFINITIVE guide to Democratic Party
accomplishments in the Trump era

The DEFINITIVE guide to Democratic Party
accomplishments in the Trump era

The DEFINITIVE guide to Democratic Party
accomplishments in the Trump era

The DEFINITIVE guide to Democratic Party
accomplishments in the Trump era

The DEFINITIVE guide to Democratic Party
accomplishments in the Trump era

The DEFINITIVE guide to Democratic Party
accomplishments in the Trump era

The DEFINITIVE guide to Democratic Party
accomplishments in the Trump era

The DEFINITIVE guide to Democratic Party
accomplishments in the Trump era

The DEFINITIVE guide to Democratic Party
accomplishments in the Trump era

The DEFINITIVE guide to Democratic Party
accomplishments in the Trump era

The DEFINITIVE guide to Democratic Party
accomplishments in the Trump era

www.ingramcontent.com/pod-product-compliance
Lightning Source LLC
Chambersburg PA
CBHW051814050726
47598CB00006B/2554